Printed in the United States of America.

Springer Literary House LLC
6260 Lavender Cloud Place
Las Vegas, Nevada 89122, USA

www.springerliteraryhouse.com

Fragments

10th Anniversary Editon

ML WISSING

ALSO BY ML WISSING

STANDALONE BOOKS

The Game
Fragments

SERIES

The World of Hinestra

Lost in Shadow (a *Reign of Shadow* novel)
A Dance of Shadow (a *Reign of Shadow* novel)

The Darkness Calls

To Hell and Back (with Amber N.P. Mays)

ANTHOLOGY

Healing Words: A Journey Through the Ladder UPP

PRAISES FOR *FRAGMENTS*

"Beautifully written with a raw expression of combat and its effects on soldiers, families, and fellow survivors. ML Wissing captures war and combat's emotional and psychological impact on a soldier's heart and soul. The raw experience conveyed takes you into the combat zone, the homecoming, and the shared reality of our soldiers alongside civilians in-country. A must-read for those who counsel veterans and other survivors of PTSD! Her personal perspective is riveting, hopeful, and celebrates life after war. I have worked with combat veterans for over three decades, and Wissing hits the PTSD nail soundly on the head. Her personal experiences will resonate with combat veterans and families alike. Her work should be required reading for all who seek to serve veterans, especially in the mental health field."

-- Jo Vaughan, M.A.

"*Fragments* is a deeply moving collection of poems. Mrs. Wissing has taken her experiences while serving our country and shared them in a beautifully eloquent fashion. I thank Mrs. Wissing for sharing her work with the world and for her service to our country."

-- Meka James, author of *Fiendish*

"Loved it! *Fragments* is a gripping compilation of poems that outline the emotional toll war has on a soldier's psyche."

-- James Brown, Jr., author of *The Long Road Home*

"Welcome home, and thank you for your service! *Fragments* is a wonderful, thought-provoking book. I bought one copy, then another for a Vietnam combat vet, then another for a different combat vet, and still another copy for a PTSD doctor at our VA. A must-read for veterans and civilians alike."

-- Rose Coop, *Disabled American Veterans Chapter 40*

"I was always kind of disappointed that the recruiter who came to my high school told me the Army couldn't accept me due to being on antidepressants. Now I wonder if I am lucky not to have served; I was spared from experiences I'd never be able to struggle against. I was never a soldier, never a warrior... but I think now I have a glimmer more of understanding."

-- reader review

ACKNOWLEDGEMENTS

I want to thank the men and women who helped make this possible, revised my writings, and furthered my ability to reach others in ways I could never have imagined.

Mrs. Marilyn Lipscomb Clark, my middle school teacher, you believed in me when no one else would. I promised you a copy if I ever published anything. I haven't forgotten.

To Dr. Sandman, who taught me to reach new horizons and challenge myself while having fun. You helped me find unseen doors in a world I thought I knew so well and gave me the courage to walk through them.

To those at the VA and those who stood by me through my various struggles during and after deployment, helping me move forward in the shadow of PTSD you've done wonders for me. You helped me understand that asking for help isn't a sign of weakness but of strength.

Silouan Green, your Ladder Upp program helped me and many others. Without it, I'm not sure this book would have ever happened. I am truly honored to have been part of something so wonderful.

Stick Vet, thank you for the resources and helping with ensuring I have the most up-to-date programs listed. I've been a fan of your work and am honored to have you take the time to discuss with me newer resources and programs that I didn't know about.

Brent, thank you for helping me grow throughout my military career and beyond. Your aid in editing the *Elite Force* scene helped it become what I always dreamed it could be. I love ya, brother.

Rakhi Verna, my wonderful editor, thank you for helping me with editing the hardest thing I've ever written. You've done wonders for me and saved me a lot of emotional heartache by taking on this task.

Dad, you've always been my hero. I love you so much. You've been an inspiration throughout my life.

Mama and hubby, I love you so much. You guys are awesome. Thank you for supporting me through so much and being understanding through it all. Your support and compassion have helped me achieve things I'd never thought possible.

DEDICATIONS

To my fellow brothers and sisters in arms past, present,
and future: thank you. IGY6.

To those who support us:
We could not do this without you. Your sacrifice does not
go unnoticed. Thank you.

To "Chief."
Fly high, brother. 'Til Valhalla.

The poem "Partners" is dedicated to Khai and Hawkeye,
you are the reason it was written.

FOREWORD

Michele [Wissing] writes about her own "fragments" and, in doing so, gives us a glimpse into the hearts and souls of those young men and women who fight our wars what motivates them to join, the traumas they face, and the struggles of leaving the war behind and coming home.

Trauma and pain left to cure deep in our souls are destructive. Trauma and pain uncovered and shared with others heal and remind us that we are not alone. Together, we can walk forward to understand the fragments and cracks we all have. As you read Michele's Fragments, not only will you see a poignant glimpse of war from a soldier's perspective, but you might also glean insights into your own fragments.

Let these powerful poems and vignettes of war remind us to never forget those who serve. As Michele so eloquently and simply states:

Rest in Peace.
Thank you, my friend.
You are not forgotten.

I pray that you will read these poems and return to them, that you will share them with others as a reminder of what it means to go to war and what it means to come home.

With much gratefulness and joy,
Silouan Green

Note from M.L. Wissing

I met Silouan Green in college through the Ladder Upp program, which used writing as a tool for healing. He is a military veteran who, after surviving a jet crash, found himself fragmented and hopeless. Since then, he has discovered his reason to live, becoming a speaker and writer who helps others heal and rebuild after crises. His inspiration helped me write about my own fragments. I am honored to have him write the foreword to my book.

Please look up his work at www.silouan.com.

WARNING

This work contains descriptions of war and loss.

If you experience symptoms of PTSD while reading, please do not hesitate to reach out to someone for support.

The Veterans Crisis Line is available 24/7:

📞 Dial 988, then press 1
💬 Chat live or text 838255

It is free and confidential you decide how much information you want to share.

The back of the book contains additional hotlines and helpful resources, updated as of the year of this book's release.

Fragments

"Our spirits are like a glass vase; unique, beautiful, and whole.
Once broken and put back together, the cracks that are the most noticeable
are not on the outside, but the inside. No matter how hard you try,
the vase will never be as whole as it once had been.

There will always be fragments left behind."

-- ML Wissing

FRAGMENTS: 10TH ANNIVERSARY EDITION

The 10th Anniversary Edition of Fragments features new poems and includes others some I wrote but did not include in the original edition, as well as newer ones composed since.

I have chosen to edit the short story scene from the unpublished Elite Force series but have also included its unedited, original form at the back of the book as a tribute to the scene that first helped me understand PTSD and the sacrifices that accompany it.

FINDING *FRAGMENTS* WITHIN

I had been back from Iraq for over ten years before the idea for this book came to me.

I decided to take a poetry writing class in college, even though I hadn't written in years. For extra credit, we could attend a poetry reading where two guest poets would be performing their work. I decided to go, and suddenly, my mind buzzed with the urge to write. I pulled out a notebook and pen, scribbling haphazardly while listening to the rhythm of the poems being read.

After the reading, I closed my notebook, put it in my bag, and went on with the rest of my day, forgetting all about it.

About two weeks later, I was going through my backpack when I came across the notebook and remembered writing something during the poetry reading. Curious, I flipped through the pages and found them covered in scattered poetry, some cohesive, some just a line or two, and others merely fragments of ideas.

What caught my attention was that they were all centered around Iraq and my experiences in the military. I realized these poems were expressions of the deep-seated emotions, memories, and feelings I had carried for years.

Our final project was a collection of poems, so I took these pieces, rewrote and organized them, and turned them in for a grade. A few classmates were impressed and encouraged me to publish them. I don't remember the grade, but after finishing the class, I couldn't let go of the idea.

I went on Facebook and asked a few friends I had served with to read the poetry and share their thoughts.

Should I try publishing something like this?

Many wrote back, saying they found it therapeutic and that, after so long, I finally had stories that were ready to be told.

Then came an interaction I will never forget.

One of my friends from the military messaged me. "I didn't know others felt this way. Is this PTSD?"

Having written many papers on the subject in college, I explained that, yes, how I described it in the book was how I experienced it, but others have different symptoms. "I think I might have PTSD."

"Okay, let's get you help."

I guided him toward getting help, providing phone numbers for contacts at the VA and offering to go with him if he needed support. He is doing much better today.

But that moment made me decide to publish my poetry to help other veterans. I hoped that when a veteran read the book, they would realize they were not the only ones who felt this way and maybe, they would seek help.

My civilian friends read it, and one of them said, "I now understand what it means when you say you are having a bad day." It helped him realize that when I said I had PTSD, it wasn't just words flashbacks were real, not something imagined.

It has been ten years since Fragments was first published, and it has reached many people since.

It has been used in programs such as Invisible Vets, Veterans Affairs groups, Disabled American Veterans, and in two schools' English programs to demonstrate how writing can help process trauma and emotions.

I once sold a copy to a congressman's aide who visited my college during our Veterans Day program.

In 2024, Fragments was featured on CBS Radio's People of Distinction in an interview with Benji Cole.

In 2025, I was chosen, interviewed, and accepted as an Honored Listee into Marquis Who's Who for my work with veterans as well as my writing and photomanipulation artwork, some of which are also based on veterans.

In republishing Fragments for its tenth anniversary, I hope to reach even more people and, possibly, get the book into bookstores and military bases to help those who need it.

I want veterans to know that help is always available. They are not alone there is support for those struggling.

You are never alone.

CONTENTS

Tastes of Sand

"When angels carry you they leave no footprints in the sand."
-- Maria Dorfner

the *elite force* scene

Around the time I was 16 or 17, I had started writing a novel series titled *Elite Force*. I was heavily influenced by my father reading Tom Clancy and W.E.B. Griffin novels, watching Alias on television, and countless other movies.

The *Elite Force* series followed a fictional black-operations squad within the Secret Service, directly involved with the President of the United States. They carried out missions that no one officially knew about.

I worked on the manuscripts every chance I had. Every scrap of paper was filled with notes about the series, and when I finally typed them up, each manuscript was over 150 pages fully formatted, they would have been much longer. Two of the books were written on my parents' computer, which crashed while I was serving in the military, resulting in the loss of both books. Luckily, one manuscript had been printed out, and it included a flashback scene that remains one of my favorite pieces I have ever written.

Since deciding to republish *Fragments* for its 10th anniversary, I felt it was time to properly edit one of my favorite pieces. To honor the scene that helped me understand sacrifice and PTSD, I have included its original, unedited text in the back of the book.

Each section of this book includes a part of that scene, in which Elite Force Agent Arthur Grant is at home, still dealing with the aftermath of a mission from years earlier. As he falls asleep after a night of heavy drinking, his mind recalls the day that changed his life forever.

Running.

Shots were being fired at his men. At him.

Arthur Grath ducked behind a trash can, one of the few lining the empty streets of this horrid little town in Bermuda, and fired back, shouting for his men to keep moving as he provided cover fire. He wondered how it had come to this.

After a known terrorist fled to Bermuda following multiple subway bombings that shut down transportation in five major U.S. cities, twelve Elite Force agents were sent to retrieve him, including Grath's best friend and partner, Mark O'Patrick. They had been tracking the terrorist for months, establishing a rapport with him on the dark web, but had never seen him in person.

During the flight over, they decided that Catherine, Mark's daughter and fellow agent, would go into a restaurant and talk to the bartender, a known affiliate of the terrorist, to gather intel on his whereabouts by posing as a buyer for stolen military weaponry.

"A group of men asking for a wanted man would be too damned noticeable," Mark had said, and Grath had to admit there was truth to that.

Unwilling to let Catherine go in alone, Grath went with her, posing as a millionaire looking to make some unsavory purchases. Catherine pretended to be Grath's new bride, an oblivious woman unaware of her husband's true business who did not speak Arabic, allowing the men to converse freely while she looked around, seemingly bored but carefully ensuring they weren't being watched too closely. Asking the right questions of the bartender proved fruitful, and they got the information they needed. Their target had a private helicopter scheduled to depart that afternoon. If they missed him now, there was no telling when they'd find him again.

It was now or never.

The Elite Force agents immediately drove their two SUVs to the airfield, where guards stopped them. Mark parked and rolled down his window to speak to the guard, smiling.

The guard shook his head, telling them in French that they had to turn around the restricted area.

"I don't understand, we are supposed to be here, just call Jea--"

"For Pete's sake," Grath snapped as he seized the second guard by the passenger-side window, yanked his arm inside, slammed his head against the car door frame, and let him go. The guard collapsed to the ground, clutching his head. Timothee shot the first guard with a silenced pistol, while Jackson shot the second, then the camera by the guard stand.

Mark showed no expression as he drove through the red-and-white wooden board blocking their entrance, their other vehicle close behind.

"Temper, temper, Grath."

"We don't have time to lose this guy."

They sped across the airfield until they spotted the helicopter warming up. Mark parked beside it and jumped out of the vehicle, with Grath behind him. The other SUV skidded to a stop, and the agents piled out, weapons drawn.

"Go! We'll take the helicopter, you get Jean-Beau!" Catherine yelled, rushing toward the helicopter with four agents.

Grath and Mark took off toward the warehouse with the remaining five agents, weapons ready.

Gunfire erupted immediately, forcing the team to scramble for cover.

"There goes the element of surprise," Grath grumbled as splintered wood rained around him.

"I think we lost that when you attacked the guard," Mark replied, glancing around the crate they hid behind. "There are three in the doorway, and they have rifles. Probably the ones you wanted to buy."

Grath pulled his rifle from his side and shrugged as he unfolded the stock. "They're just demonstrating they work. Can't purchase bad goods, you know." Bracing himself on the crate, he sat up and returned fire. "Get moving! I'll cover you!"

Two agents sprinted toward another pile of crates. They gave a thumbs-up and began providing cover as one of the shooters dropped, while a second ducked back inside the building.

Mark rushed forward, staying low as he took position behind a crate.

Grath nodded as the man he shot collapsed, spotting movement deeper inside the warehouse. But he couldn't see who or what it was from his angle.

"Found him!" Mark shouted, glancing through the doorway. He rushed to the side of the door, peeking around the edge and stepping over the bodies of the fallen gunmen. He fired a shot and ducked back, waiting. After a moment, he pushed inside, another agent following close behind.

"Damn it! Don't take him alone!" Grath swore, looking at the three agents beside him. "Call Catherine's group and let them know what's going on. Johnson, you're with me."

Hearing Johnson's footsteps behind him, Grath sprinted toward the warehouse.

A NATION IN CHAOS

I remember.

I remember the day the Twins fell.
Proud before brought low to the ground
by an act of cowardice. Of terror.

Lives snuffed out like so many candles.
Terror alight like so many flames,
burning through our minds, our hearts.

No one felt safe.
No one felt sure.
Everyone mourned and suffered as one.

Flags were flown, songs were sung.
Everyone became patriotic.
They should have been from the beginning.

I signed up,
joined the military.
Became a soldier.

And we
became a nation.

If only we had remembered
we were one before.

THE LESSON

10 September 2001,
I ran away from home,
fled to another city so I
could be at work the next day.

I was so proud of myself.
I can do this! I'll show them!
I stayed with my friend at her video store,
laughing and thinking I was an adult.

My father walked in,
told me I would have to stay in a hotel.
I got a room,
and I stayed the night.

The next morning,
I watched the towers fall
from the television in the hotel lobby.

Months later,
my father asked me why I ran away.
"Because I was angry," I said.

He looked at me
and asked why the terrorists attacked the Twins.
"Because they hate Americans."

"No," came his reply, and he looked at me.
"Because they were angry.
See how something so small… can do so much?"

I will remember the lesson all my days.

VOLUNTEERS

We volunteered,
unbidden.

There were no guns pointed
at our heads,
no threats,
no promises,

as our unshaking hands
held pens of black ink,
and we spoke the oath,
signing our lives away
to a cause greater than ourselves.

TOGETHER WE STAND

The towers fell
over and over on our television sets,
grinding the lesson into everyone's head.

Eyes turned to visions of horror,
to nightmares of terror of real life.

Higher and higher, fear and anger grew,
that everyone was out to get us
in reality, or only in our minds.

We wanted vengeance. We wanted justice.
Everyone demanded different things.

Steadily, we were sent to war,
through times of strife over sandy oceans,
across the world and far away
never forgetting the purpose of our mission:
to defend our home, our families.

MEMOIRS OF A SOLDIER

I look at the sand that lays
all around my feet.
I close my eyes and tell myself
it's not reality.

No convincing is good enough,
no matter how hard you try,
and all the damned sand is there
it makes you want to cry.

How did I end up here?
I still remember that day
when I wanted to be better
than those who threw their lives away.

I stood and raised my hand
(it made my parents so proud!),
I swore an oath of allegiance,
before them, before God.

It seems so long ago
that I was in training,
learning how to be tough and fight
even when it was windy and raining.

Learning a whole new job,
going to a new school,
going home to see
the people that you knew.

The smiling faces,
a couple thanks and shakes of hands,
a few points and stares
they didn't understand.

What it means to wear the greens
or the desert-colored tan,
to go and fight for freedom
in a strange, faraway land.

What it means to see our flag
proudly wave above,
or read the words of those
who send you their love.

The people here are my family too,
my brothers and sisters in arms.
We watch each other's backs,
protect each other from harm.

We know why it is said
that freedom is not free.
It may not mean anything to you,
but it means a lot to me.

Smells of Gunpowder

"Older men declare war. But it youth that must fight and die."
-- Herbert Hoover

Mark was taking fire from behind cover when Grath burst through the hangar door and rushed behind a stack of cargo covered with a tarp. Providing cover fire for his partner, Grath pushed forward as the rest of his team caught up.

Shooters hidden behind equipment in the hangar popped up like groundhogs, taking shots at them. The Elite Force agents quickly picked them off one by one until some grew smart enough to stop exposing themselves.

The clinking of an object rolling across the floor sent them scrambling for cover.

"Grenade!"

They dove behind whatever they could find, pressing low to the ground just as the grenade exploded. Debris rained down upon them, and for a moment, the world was silent except for the high-pitched whine that would fade with time.

Grath reloaded, scanning for the agents. He spotted

Mark rushing toward the open back door.

A bullet whizzed past Grath's head, tearing a chunk from the shelf behind him. He spun, firing as men with rifles stormed in from the entrance, attempting to ambush them from behind. Focused on returning fire, Grath didn't notice that Mark had already rushed out the back of the warehouse.

When the gunfire ended and the attackers lay dead, Grath turned his attention back to the mission. He looked around for his teammates before sprinting forward, weapon ready.

The street outside the warehouse was eerily empty civilians had likely fled at the first sound of gunfire and explosions. Staying behind cover to avoid exposing themselves unnecessarily, the agents took off toward the distant echo of gunshots.

Catherine looked up from zip-tying the helicopter pilot when she heard the explosion, glancing at her team leader.

"Catherine, you and Jackes stay with the pilot and co-pilot. The rest of you on me," Trevis ordered, grabbing another rifle magazine from the SUV before sprinting across the airfield toward the thick smoke billowing into the blue sky.

When they reached the grenade blast site, one of the wounded men informed them that Mark and the others were up ahead. Without hesitation, they pushed forward, running alongside the building.

HORIZON OVER THE SAND

The sand stretches for miles.
It gets everywhere.

Footprints fade as fast as the wind blows.
The sun burns the skin.
Vision blurs as the sand swirls, drawing closer.

Bullets fly like buzzing bees.
Screams and shouts heard and unheard.

Wounds deepen, fester.
The white sand turns red.

Silence prevails over the horizon
as the wind washes away the scene,
the sand stretching for miles once more.

MILES TO GO

Feet fall heavily,
breaking the sand,
making tracks
that quickly fade with the wind.

Pulling their rifles closer,
wrapping themselves in its cold companionship.
The wind and sand sting their eyes and skin,
young faces barely bearing a beard.

Aching muscles, hearts longing for home,
arms missing a form to wrap around,
bellies hungering for warm food,
legs and faces numb.

They walk, ignoring it all.
The platoon keeps moving.
They walk.

Miles to go.

THROUGH IRAQ, DECEMBER 2004

Sharp cold stings the nose with the scent of ice.
Frozen water chills and rests upon the ground,
unseen beneath the feet of those walking to and from.

A pale white speck lands upon brown sand.

Earth-colored boots and ground-colored pants
the only movement in the cold, barren land,
stretching out for miles to pale horizons unseen.
Mud-caked soles tell of long journeys.

Movement stops as another white drop lands on black
metal.
Tanned hands move to stay warm.
Eyes rise to the heavens, wondering, surprised.
Could it truly be snow?

FEAR

Heart thumping,
adrenaline pumping,
hands frozen at your sides.

Fight or flight

you decide.

WAITING TO DIE

The bunker's concrete front and back.
Above, a ceiling of the same gray.
Five inches thick.
Thousands of sandbags around it,
cushioning shrapnel from explosions.

The first explosion farther away.
Another explosion.
Closer.

Stoop, can't stand.
Sit, can't lie.
More soldiers pour in.
Iraqis enter from the other side.

Huddled together.
Forty-five-pound bulletproof vests and rifles.
Stoop, can't stand.
Sit, can't lie.

Another explosion.
Closer.

Air grows stuffy
the taste of native odor,
of bodies unbathed for months.
Pressed together tighter.
More people.

Another explosion.
Closer.

Lame jokes.
Forced laughter.
The beeping of a Game Boy game.
Another explosion.

Prayer muttered in English.
A pair of eyes glare at the Iraqis.
Someone says we should take them outside
shoot them all.
This is all their fault.

Another explosion.
Closer still.

Snap at him to shut up.
Anger and fear intermingle in the air.
A Game Boy beep signifies a level up.

Another explosion.

Swears spat out.
Lame jokes and forced laughter.
The explosions grow closer.

Another. Another. Another.
Like a giant walking closer.
Will the bunker hold?

Another.

The sudden sound of a building,
a hundred feet or less away,
exploding as it is hit.

Pieces fall like rain.
Breaths leave lungs in unison.
The air grows still.

Another explosion shatters the silence.
Closer.

Another. Another.

You pray.
You continue waiting;
Waiting to die.

Visions of Loss

"Greater love has no one than this: to lay down one's life for another man."
-- John 15:13

Grath ran around the corner just in time to see Mark fall to his knees, his chest and abdomen exploding with red spray. He ducked behind cover as their target turned and fired at him, chunks of paint and stone flying off the corner near his face. Leaning around, he returned fire as the rest of the team caught up.

The target took cover in a doorframe, and Grath seized the opportunity to rush forward, slipping behind a dumpster alongside a building he needed a better angle to engage. The terrorist stepped out of the doorframe, aiming his AK-47 just as Grath leaned to fire.

Suddenly, the target jerked, spun slightly, and stumbled halfway through the doorway, his rifle dropping from his hands.

Movement caught Grath's eye as the rest of the team advanced, rifles up, using cover to close in.

Mark had rolled onto his side, his Desert Eagle locked on the target, protecting his partner despite his wounds.

As the team approached, he lay back, his chest rising and falling with heavy breaths.

The rest of the team secured the site while Grath rushed to where Jean-Beau had fallen. The mission always came first if the site wasn't secure, they could all die.

Grath looked down in disgust at the terrorist who had caused so much harm to his country and now his partner. The scumbag was dead, his empty eyes staring up. Grath kicked the man's weapon far from his hand, then pulled out his pistol and shot him twice in the chest and once between the eyes.

"There. Now I know you're dead."

He left the building at a sprint.

Mark lay on his back as the others tried to remove his armored vest, carefully pulling it over his head to assess the damage. His undershirt was soaked in blood. The vest's ceramic plate had stopped the first bullets, but two had made it through: one to the chest, the other to the abdomen.

Grath knelt beside his partner. "MEDIC!"

The young medic looked up from Mark's other side.

"I'm right here, Grath," he said, pressing a piece of plastic over the wound. Another agent handed him tape, and they quickly sealed three sides down. "It sounds like it went through a lung. The other shot is in the abdomen. God... he must have hit the liver or another vital organ. He's bleeding too much internally. He's not going to make it."

Grath snapped his pistol up, pointing it at the medic's face.

The air around them went still.

"You do something about it," he ordered, "or I will fucking shoot you right now. Do it."

"Grath, I; I can't do anything out here," the medic stammered. "I have nothing to perform surgery with. No tools, no--"

"Here," Grath snapped open his Gerber multi-tool one-handed and shoved it at the man, his pistol still steady in his other hand.

The medic, along with everyone else gathered around, stared at him in shock. A few agents took a step back. Some exchanged glances, hands on their holsters, waiting for someone to decide what to do next.

Grath never took his eyes off the medic. "You fix whatever the hell is wrong with him. That's my partner."

HERO

You call me a hero?
I, who locked and loaded every morning,
worrying I'd have to take a life.

I, who shot a child, not knowing if the object they held
was a grenade or a piece of fruit,
but I had to act to preserve myself and my comrade.

I, who listened to a mother's wailing,
a father's angry words as we tried to pay them fifty dollars
for killing their daughter, who ran into the street during a
firefight.

Fifty dollars.
The price of a life…
is that what life is worth these days?

You call me a hero?
I, who lay awake, wondering if I was going away to war,
leaving behind the better life I built friends, family, and
freedom.

I, who was ordered to shoot to kill
when all I wanted was to sit and talk,
to share a cup of spiced chai and end this like men.

I, who kept shooting while injured,
who held comrades, friends, brothers, and sisters
as they lay dying in my arms.

Telling them they would be all right,
lying to them, hiding my own tears and fears,
as the last light faded from their eyes, the last fell.

You call me a hero?

There are no heroes.

ODE TO THE HEART

Oh, small, strong one,
how you've been beaten,
stepped on, pushed around,
neglected, sacrificed
yet you live,
somehow.

Memories of losses
dwell in your mind,
in your veins,
like a mother's arms
after losing her babe.

Betrayals and pain,
fresh wounds that bleed,
leaving you lying still,
like so much dead meat.

IT SHOULD HAVE BEEN ME

It should have been me
lying under the sheet,
so another life would have been saved
by my actions, my love of brotherhood.

It should have been me,
under the draped flag,
so your family would not have to suffer;
I had no family waiting for me at home.

Yet you are gone, and I am here,
tracing my name on my dog tags slowly,
as if it were my name on the stone.

I hide my head under the blanket,
pray it all stops.
I fight not to breathe in the air you should be tasting.

It should have been me.

BROKEN

The things we left behind were replaced
with visions we cannot forget.
Pieces of us never returned,
buried in unmarked graves,
taunting us as ghosts
we cannot exorcise.

SURVIVOR'S TALE

The scariest sound I've ever heard
was my own heartbeat.
The worst pain I've ever felt
was taking in air to breathe.
The most horrible thing I've ever seen
was looking back at me in the mirror.

Nothing seems the same anymore;
nothing will ever be the same.

For I've done the unthinkable,
the unimaginable.

I survived.

I'm still here.
This isn't Darwin's theory
survival of the fittest.
This isn't *Survivor* or *Big Brother*.

This is reality.
The drama known as Life.
Showing seven days a week,
twenty-four hours a day.

We're built to survive.
We've learned to strive to win.

But did anyone notice
if you survive,
you still lose?

AFTER THE BATTLE

She walks among the silent earth,
carefully stepping around the lifeless forms
that litter the blood-soaked ground.

She looks at the dead, the wounded, the afraid
each with eyes that carry all emotion
or none at all.

In her hand is a long rod,
a scythe at one end,
a cross at the other.

She represents the balance
between good and evil,
right and wrong,
life and death.

Looking around now,
even she knows not who was right…
or who was wrong.

But it is not for her to justify.
Not today.

She walks and cuts the cords
that bind body and soul
mercy to those too injured to go on,
a nightmare to those barely hurt.

She takes them at random,
picking souls as one might pick flowers.

She walks away silently,
with another bouquet for God.

HIDDEN FEARS

I'm staying in the shadows now,
never in the sun,
hiding from all the fear
that came when the war began.

I stay within four walls now,
I don't go out at all.
No one understands me
or my tears that fall.

No one's there to calm my fears
or silence the images in my head,
the ones that haunt me every night
when I'm alone in bed.

I'm too afraid to go too far
outside my bedroom door.
I just can't do all the things
I loved so much before.

I feel like I'm going crazy,
like my head is not attached.
God put His thumbprint on my heart
then the Devil left a scratch.

TELL ME

Doctor, tell me I'm not going crazy,
tell me I'm not insane.
Tell me the things I feel
aren't wrong inside my brain.

Tell me why I'm scared
when everyone else feels safe.
Tell me that's why I stayed inside
instead of going out today.

When the sun is shining bright,
I'm inside with the curtains drawn.
I sit and stare and wait
until the Sandman comes.

Tell me why I'm nervous,
tell me why I'm scared.
I keep my things with me,
yet I feel so unprepared.

The people around me are foes,
but they were once my friends.
Everything seems to have changed,
and my world feels like will end.

I am so much jumpier now,
scared of shadows others don't see.
Doctor, tell me there is a cure
for what is wrong with me.

NIGHTMARE

Wake up screaming,
dreaming of the past.
Huddle in the blankets,
pray it won't last.

Turn on the light,
quickly look around.
Unseen assailants gone,
only shadows to be found.

Tears in your eyes,
threatening to rain.
You keep telling yourself
you aren't going insane.

Breathe in, breathe out,
heart slowing down.
Want to go back to sleep,
but keep looking around.

I watch as the world
shatters beneath my feet.
I am suspended in the air,

feeling nothing.

Sounds of Echoes

"I want someone to pinch me so I can feel something, anything. I'm sick of this numbness, of feeling so alone and outside of everything, but I know it's too dangerous to wake up."
-- Carol Matas

A hand touched Grath's arm, which was still pointing at the medic, and slowly lowered it much to the relief of the group, who also lowered their weapons slightly. One of the members began radioing for the other team to bring the helicopter.

Grath looked down at Mark's hand, then at his partner, who smiled weakly.

"We got him, didn't we?"

Grath smiled in return.

"We sure did, man. Hang in there. The doc's going to fix you up."

Mark coughed and winced; his eyes full of pain when he looked at Grath.

"Take care of Catherine for me?"

"You aren't going anywhere. Just hang in there for us. They're getting the chopper right now. It'll be okay soon. Just hang in there."

Mark coughed and closed his eyes. When he opened

them again, they were filled with unshed tears.

"Say it."

Grath stared, his voice lost. He finally found it, and when he spoke, it came out pinched and strained as he fought back tears.

"I promise, Mark, I will keep her safe. But you aren't going anywhere, you hear me? So shut up and breathe."

He turned his head, pretending to scan the area, refusing to let the tears fall.

When he looked down again, Mark's eyes were staring straight ahead, the light inside them fading. Grath put his hand over his partner's face and closed his eyes.

The medic checked for a pulse and shook his head in defeat. The other members lowered their heads, preparing themselves for their next tasks.

Footsteps rushing toward them made Grath spin around, pistol drawn and ready.

When he saw Catherine running toward them with the rest of the team, he stepped beside Mark. A look of horror flashed across her face as she recognized the fallen member. She ran faster toward them, yelling, everything else forgotten.

Grath holstered his pistol and rushed to Catherine, grabbing her around the shoulders and guiding her away from the team. He held her as she fought to break free, yelling at each of them, her fists pounding against him.

Grath tightened his arms around her, stopping her blows against his chest, whispering in her ear as she dropped to her knees, screaming.

"Not here, not now."

Overhead, the sound of the helicopter grew closer.

FRAGMENTS OF THE SKY

Fragments falling from the sky
steel, sparks, and fire,
like rain from a burst cloud.
The sound of explosion so high,
yet so deep.

Dive to get behind cover,
dive to get low to the ground.
Damn the sand in your mouth,
damn the scrapes from harsh rocks
dive to get safe.

People glance at you,
wondering what's wrong with you.
Why aren't you normal?
Why are you like that?
Why can't you be like everyone else?

Slowly stand, brush off the sand.
No… grass.
Grass?

Look for your weapon, the enemy.
Look around… where are you?

The faces around you staring,
the voices whispering.
Try not to look embarrassed.
Laugh off your shaking.
Just pretend it will be all right.

Damn the Fourth of July.

TO MY KNEES

The sound of a firework sends me to my knees;
it is the only way I won't fall down,
the only way I won't dive to the concrete beneath me.

I can't move.
My legs refuse to work,
my arms, my heart frozen.

My sergeant comes over,
kneels beside me, not touching, not laughing.

"Where are you right now?"

His soft voice is gentle.
He doesn't see you as you do -- a coward.
He understands.

He has been there before, in your boots.
Scared before, away from home before, reliving it before.
Now he is through that. But he knows.

My voice shakes.

"I am in a concrete bunker, waiting to die."

Another firework. Try to get lower.

"Come sit by me.
You'll be all right. You must hear the noise,
train yourself not to run from it anymore."

I give him a look of doubt.

"I was once there too. It is all right.
You can do this. I promise."

I sit, tears streaming down my face.
A worry stone of a closed knife in my hand,
rubbing the handle over and over and over.

Others see. No one laughs.
Some sit beside me in silent support.
I ask myself, when memories creep
"Where are you right now?"

PARTNERS

I entered this life not knowing where my journey would
take me.
Along the way, I found a partner.

Separate, we were soldiers, fighters.
Separate, we felt alone.
Together, we were more.

I could count on my partner no matter what,
and they could count on me.

When they were happy, so was I.
When they were sad, I comforted them.
When they were scared, I chased the fears away.

I didn't always understand why.
But my partner needed me
that, I understood.

When news came that my partner was ill, I was there for
them,
and I tried to make them happy.

When my partner's strides grew slower and weaker,
I was their strength.

I never realized that sometimes, I was the only reason
my partner fought to hold on.

In my last breaths, I'll pray my partner finds another
partner,
one who loves them as much as I do.

We were never just partners.
We were never just soldier and service animal.

We are one.

----

*Note: This poem is dedicated to the bond between service members and service
animals. It is written to be read from either perspective, and I invite you to
experience it from both.*

HALL OF HEROES I

The silence follows the *shhh* of the hospital doors closing.
The smell is overwhelming;
fear, pain, horror, shame, and anger assault the senses.
Yes, these things have smells.

These are things the primal mind never forgets.
The sharp sting of antibacterial cleaners burns the eyes,
makes the mind want to retreat far away.
The clean air is too heavy.

Hushed breathing, silent regrets, and burdened memories
weigh down the very atmosphere.
Moving down the bleached hall is suddenly difficult
a struggle to keep moving forward.

The waiting rooms are filled with ghosts
of men and women who paid their dues and then some,
who now sit and wait in long lines for their time to come.
The warriors they once were, trapped inside fleshy tombs.

Their voices whisper of old wounds,
their minds replay memories unsaid.
Their eyes speak the loudest of all
foreign languages to all but each other.

HALL OF HEROES II

Breathe in. Breathe out.
Try to stop the mental screaming,
the primal sounds of the subconscious
slowly fading to black only to return later.

We are dying inside our forsaken husks of bodies,
on white sheets of bed,
like chrysalises lying on the cold earth.
But we will never emerge as butterflies.

We and our wings are broken
torn, forgotten, crippled
shattered fragments gathered in
wheelchairs of our own design.

Fresh, old memories trip through the mind,
tearing holes,
bloody wounds;
the brain left like so much dead meat.

We are changed.
Forever.
But we remember.

We remember.

THE BATTLE TO LIVE AGAIN

Metal needles and plastic tubing
become chains anchoring
to bedsides, therapy horrible pain and relief.

What a curse and a blessing to be alive,
a double-sided coin spinning on its edge;
one movement can make it fall.

The nurses take care not to bump the table,
for fear of jolting the water cup
so you can swallow your medications,
just as you do every morning.

The sun slaps you through the window,
the birds mock your existence,
reminding you that you are in hell.

Your brothers and sisters lay dying,
somewhere far away,
blood soaking the sand around them.

And here you lay, drinking Valium-and-water cocktails
from little paper cups without little paper umbrellas,
another concoction to drown the pain.

If you close your eyes hard enough,
you can feel the sand, hear the blasts of gunfire;
it calms you more than any drug ever will.

They won't understand.
They don't understand.
They never will.

It calls to you: the battle, the blood, the brothers.
All you want is to go back
and finally be alive once again.

HUG

Arms wrapped around me
in the middle of the fight,
carrying me from the monsters
and closer to the light.

Tears fall upon the shoulder
pressed against my cheek,
strength in torso and heart
to fall upon when I feel weak.

Companionship and love
hold the sneaking shadows at bay.
The still air is quiet
no words we need to say.

In the grasp of memories,
a silent cry for help.
The comfort of a hug reminds me
I am not by myself.

----

*Note: I wrote this poem two days after experiencing my first PTSD attack in years during an **IPFW Ladder UPP™ Creative Writing Group** meeting.*

It caught me completely by surprise, leaving me so rattled that the other members noticed. Sensing how I felt, one of them walked over and hugged me silently, holding me for as long as I needed.

At that moment, that hug spoke more to me than any words ever could.

THE COINS ON THE HEADSTONE

When walking through a graveyard,
and you see a coin on stone,
please do a favor
and leave the coin alone.

It may just be a sight
for which you are unprepared,
but let me tell you why
those coins are sitting there.

Those coins are more
than just change left alone;
they actually tell a story
about the hero beneath the stone.

A penny is a small,
simple action like a wave.
It means you have visited
and stood beside the grave.

A nickel holds
a little more meaning.
It means you knew the soldier
when you both were in basic training.

If one knew the soldier
and served with them some time,
that is why they
would go and leave a dime.

If you see a quarter
upon the stone of death,
it means the person was there
when the soldier drew their last breath.

So when you see a coin,
pay respect and walk on by.
The coins on the headstone tell all:
"You were here, and so was I."

VETERANS' DAY SPEECH 2019

One of the Disabled American Veterans chapters invited me to speak at the Veterans' Day Parade Ceremony in Fort Wayne, Indiana, on November 9, 2019. It was a profound honor and remains one of my proudest moments and favorite memories.

This is the speech I gave that day, unedited from its original version.

When I was asked to write a speech for today, my first words were, "Great, who is going to give it?"

"The one who is writing it."

I thought Gerard [a friend in the Disabled American Veterans Chapter 40] was kidding; after all, what was I supposed to talk about?

"Talk about what Veterans Day means to you."

You would think that that is an easy subject for me I'm third-generation military, married to a veteran, and a veteran myself. But this is actually the hardest speech I've had to write.

You see, in my family, every day is Veterans Day.

Every day, you remember that nothing you have would be possible without veterans.

I lived on military bases, where your neighbors were military, and your friends' parents at least one of them were military. You appreciated them every day.

So, this has had me struggling to write this for about a

month or so.

All of my life, I have been surrounded by superheroes.

Not the ones you'd normally think of today, found in comic books or movies but mine were real.

The superheroes in my world don't have capes or bright colors. They wore dog tags, sang cadences, and were always there to protect you.

They were the police you waved to, who waved back.

They were the ones who fought fires and came when you were injured.

They were the ones in uniforms.

My first hero was my dad.

He is a huge inspiration in my life. He was in the Army, and I wanted to be like him. He taught me the importance of believing in myself, having confidence, and sometimes, faking it until you make it.

So, let me tell you a story.

My dad was the NBC NCOIC for Tropic Thunder.

For those who have no idea what I just said, don't worry it basically means that he was the person in charge of the chemicals in his unit at Schofield Barracks, Hawaii.

So, there is this thing called CS gas, which is basically tear gas. It burns the lungs, makes the face and exposed skin red and itchy, kills the sinuses all-around bad-smelling stuff. It's used to break up riots.

My dad worked with it all the time and would tell us stories of the "CS chamber" a large room filled with gas that soldiers enter to test their gas masks and build confidence in their equipment.

My dad always spoke of teaching in those chambers; he'd take off his mask and talk normally, saying the soldiers could do the same if they wished. Some did only to end up coughing, gagging, and putting their masks back on. Eventually, everyone had to remove their masks at least once in the chambers.

But my dad said he spoke normally and had no problems with it.

Why was that?

Because he was immune to CS gas.

I tell you that story to tell you this one.

When I was 12 and in 7th grade, we had open-air schools in Hawaii. The hallways had roofs but no walls.

One day, the first bell of the day rang, then the last bell. We had no idea what was going on, but the air smelled and tasted strange like pepper, but not quite.

We were evacuated with notes for our families, and word spread… we'd been tear-gassed.

Ha! I thought. I am immune, like my dad.

After all, that's how science works, right?

Speaking of science, let me tell you about another of my heroes.

Don't worry we'll get back to the CS gas story and my dad.

So enters my second hero, Richard Dean Anderson, a.k.a. MacGyver.

He was this amazing agent of the fictional Phoenix Foundation who taught me to think outside the box, use science and knowledge to get out of situations, and strive to learn something new every day.

I absolutely fell in love with him, and at a young age, I wanted to marry him.

I lived in Hawaii for a time, and I wanted to work with whales. I wanted to work with science. I wanted to help protect animals, especially after watching MacGyver fight against rhino poachers in Africa. Watching Free Willy only cemented my love for marine life, and I dreamed about being a marine biologist.

There are hundreds of reasons why people don't go after their childhood dreams.

I mean, come on, you were a kid, right? You must be this high to ride your dream? Maybe your dream was silly like wanting to be a frog or something. Or maybe it was just too out of this world, like becoming an astronaut. Or maybe people poked fun at you for it, so you stashed it away in the back of your brain, hiding it under some old algebra formulas still rummaging around in there.

When I was a kid, I wanted to be tons of things because the world was pretty and shiny and new, and opportunity was everywhere.

I wanted to be a military lawyer for the Navy because they had the cool white dresses for their uniforms.

I wanted to play the ukulele, be an artist, a singer, and a writer.

A lot of people told me I wouldn't amount to anything or that I couldn't do it.

I began studying reading books, watching shows

anything and everything I could to learn about my dreams.

As luck would have it, of course, I learned a few things.

For one, the actor who played MacGyver, Richard Dean Anderson, had absolutely no clue who I was.

Biology was awesome until I discovered I would have to dissect things, probably the very animals I wanted to study and protect.

I took art classes in school, found out I had some talent, but I was no professional.

And my dad was the one who accidentally CS'd my school; the wind had changed direction.

When September 11th happened, we knew my father could be called back into the military.

I secretly decided that if he went, I would go as well to help and protect him. I wanted to make sure that he would be all right, that my hero would still be here for my mother and sister. But in the months that followed, I entertained the thought of joining the military myself.

He was never recalled, but the day after Christmas, I joined the Army.

My mom thought I was joking.

Here I am, this smart-ass 19-year-old at 116 pounds; I had to get a waiver because I was underweight for the Army.

Everyone told me I couldn't do it when I told them I had joined. Everyone, including family, asked me, "Aren't you too weak?"

My drill sergeant became a hero to me; he never gave up on me. He pushed me to be my best, even though I frustrated him.

I couldn't run due to shin splints.

I'd injured my knee.

I couldn't hit the broad side of a barn when shooting.

But I never gave up so he didn't give up on me.

The gas chamber I walked in like I owned the place. After all, I was partially immune, right?

Inside the gas chamber, there were gray cement walls, a ceiling, and a floor. There was one light, and thick black smoke billowed from CS grenades on the floor, making it impossible to see in front of you.

It was claustrophobic and filled with the unknown.

They had us take off our masks and recite "Mary Had a Little Lamb," our last name, and our Social Security number.

I was proud of myself I had done it all in one breath out, so I didn't inhale any gas.

Others didn't think of that and were choking and coughing by the time they said a word or two.

On the way out the door, we had to take off our masks and wait in line to leave the chamber. I was second in line. The soldier behind me dropped his mask, and we had to stop, waiting until he found it.

With no mask on, I ran out of breath. So, I took a big intake of gas and rushed out when I could, coughing and choking.

But I had done it; I had survived the gas chamber.

Remember that childhood dream I had? The one about being a lawyer?

I served as an Army Judge Advocate General (JAG) paralegal from 2002 to 2009. I went to Kuwait, Iraq, and served in different states. I helped lock some very bad people behind bars, and I helped save people's careers some due to my decisions alone.

I loved my job. Not only had I punished bad guys, but I also stood for victims. I made sure that those who harmed them were prosecuted.

So, last year, [2018] I mentioned to my father that I was immune to CS, and he began laughing.

"Kiddo, you never paid attention in the chamber where the instructor stood, did you? There is an X on the floor where the instructor stands. Above that is fresh air being pumped in. What happens when a gas is pumped in and hits a rounded surface like the top of your head?"

Thank you, MacGyver I knew the answer from learning science with him.

"It makes a cone…."

And then it hit me.

My dad had been breathing fresh air safely in the chamber. He was never immune, which meant I was never immune either.

I felt like a giant idiot. I had walked in with so much confidence that I never even considered I could be wrong.

My heroes taught me a great deal how to believe in myself, how to use science and reasoning to get out of situations, how to walk into the unknown and tell myself I'd be fine. How to not give up even when the world is telling you to.

When I go somewhere and see a veteran's hat, I see my hero. When I walk into the VA, I see heroes lining the hallways, sitting in the chairs.

I still get nervous sometimes when I approach a veteran to thank them for their service because all I can see are the heroes I grew up around men and women I cannot hold a candle to.

I'm not a hero. I am not one of the many men and women who stand out in the crowd today those who truly deserve that term and so much more.

But I am someone who wants to help my heroes.

In college, I was at a poetry reading, and my brain would not stop buzzing, so I grabbed a pen and paper. When I looked at the paper weeks later, I discovered poems about the military and my time in Iraq my PTSD coming out after years of silence.

On September 11, 2015, the collection became my first book, Fragments, which was published. It is a book that has helped people understand PTSD and has shown veterans that they aren't alone. It has also helped civilians gain a better understanding of what it is like to be a veteran.

I'm working on books to help college officials understand veteran students better and another to help employers understand veteran employees.

I keep in contact with veterans I've even assisted some in getting help for their PTSD and spoken to those who were on the edge, ready to jump.

I have turned the lessons my heroes taught me into a crusade to help them in return.

So, go out and thank a hero someone you look up to.

Face your problems with knowledge and confidence.

The world is a CS chamber that can make you stumble, blind, and scared.

Be immune to it, and know you aren't alone.

Your heroes are always there with you.

Thank you.

THANK YOU

I did not know you personally,
but you were my brother.

I never shared a drink or a laugh with you,
but you were my friend.

There is a bond between soldiers that can never be broken
not even by death.

Rest in peace.
Thank you, my friend.
You are not forgotten.

This is a poem I sent to the families of fallen soldiers, along with a photo manipulation of their loved one in uniform, set against the flag and the Constitution, featuring their military branch's creed and seal, with the words "Never Forgotten."

It is a personal project I began in honor of the fallen member and their family's sacrifice.

It is a small comfort to me and, I pray, to their families.

AFTERWORD AND RESOURCES

I suffered from Post-Traumatic Stress for years after returning from Iraq in 2005. I sought help from my unit's medical team while deployed and later went to the VA hospital in the States for therapy and counselling because I was still experiencing issues.

I still do, sometimes, to this day.

I have lost friends and fellow servicemembers to PTSD, those we wished had gotten help and support. It is not the easiest thing to do; but for those who do, I will always support you.

Please do not hesitate to seek help.

Veteran Centers
(specifically, the ones run by RCS Readjustment Counseling Services)
Provides free counseling for all active duty and combat Veterans. This is a free resource but is widely unknown.

Veterans Suicide and Crisis Lifeline

Call 988, Press 1
Text 838255

Available 24/7. English and Spanish

https://988lifeline.org

22 Til None

https://www.22untilnone.org

A volunteer group working 24/7 dedicated to helping veterans and their families. They are a grassroots movement encouraging others to help make a monthly event where on the 22nd of every month, you call a veteran you know to check in with them.

Warrior PATHH

www.bouldercrest.org

Provides training to transform struggles into strength and thrive in the aftermath of trauma. Warrior PATHH — Progressive and Alternative Training for Helping Heroes — is based on the science of Posttraumatic Growth (PTG).

War Vet Call Center

1-877-927-8387
Available 24/7

Team comprised of veterans from several eras and family members of veterans.

Women Veteran Call Center

1-855-VA-WOMEN (1-855-829-6636)

Also can chat online anonymously

8am to 10pm ET, M-F
8am to 10pm ET, Saturday

Lifeline for Vets

888-777-4443

Speak to other veterans about your military service, needing assistance, or just to have someone to talk to.

Tragedy Assistance Program for Survivors (TAPS)

800-959-8277
Available 24/7

Provides compassionate care and resources to those grieving the loss of a military loved one, at no cost to the surviving families and loved ones.

ELITE FORCE – UNEDITED

This is the full, unedited version of the short scene from the Elite Force series that I began writing at sixteen years of age. It was included in the first edition of *Fragments* in 2015.

Running.

Shots being fired at the group of men he was with. At him.

There was no escape, no matter where they ran. He ducked behind a trash can, one of the few that lined the empty streets of this horrid little town in Bermuda, and fired a few shots back. Grath yelled to one of the men to run as he provided cover fire. He wondered how this had gotten this far.

It was supposed to be a mission to retrieve information on a known terrorist who had fled to Bermuda to escape the military after bombing a number of subway stations, shutting down transportation for five major cities across the United States. When he fled, the President sent some of the Elite Force into Bermuda, where it was determined he had taken refuge. Mark O'Patrick, Grath's best friend and partner, was assigned to the mission as well, along with Mark's daughter and fellow Elite Force Operative, Catherine O'Patrick.

Grath had been in charge of that mission and had decided that, as a female, Catherine should be the one to walk into the restaurant for the terrorist; a group of men asking for a wanted man would be too damned noticeable. She agreed and walked inside with him, posing as a newlywed young wife to an older millionaire who was there on vacation.

They had discovered their target (Grath had forgotten his name over the years) had been there and had a private helicopter set to leave that afternoon. They learned this from a bartender whom they had long ago marked as one of the target's supporters when they were briefed at headquarters.

The Elite Force immediately drove their two provided SUVs to the airfield, where they were stopped by guards. Speaking quickly in French, Mark tried to talk them into letting the group inside, using the cover story of the couple on vacation the other SUV behind them contained the couple's bodyguards. It was Grath who finally got them in by grabbing the guard by the passenger-side window, yanking his shirt, and pulling his arm back quickly, slamming the guard's head against the car door frame. He let go of the guard, who fell to the ground, clutching his head.

Mark showed no expression as he stepped on the gas and drove through the red-and-white wooden board blocking their entrance, with the other vehicle close behind.

They sped across the airfield until they spotted the helicopter warming up. Mark parked beside it and jumped out of the vehicle, Grath right behind him. The other SUV pulled to a stop, and members piled out as well, weapons drawn.

Catherine rushed to take over the helicopter with four other members of the Elite Force, while the three remaining men ran with Grath and Mark to find the target in the hangar.

Grath ran with Mark outside of the hangar, where he crouched behind a crate and gave hand signals to the rest of the group, who nodded.

At the signal, they rushed into the hangar, two at a time, immediately receiving fire after yelling in French that they were United States agents. Mark had gone up before Grath and saw the terrorist making a run for it through another doorway.

Yelling to Grath that he had found him, he took off after the running man.

Grath shouted back to Mark to wait for him and another member before taking the terrorist alone and barked orders to the group with him having them call Catherine's group to let them know what was going on and ordering one member to go with him and Mark.

Hearing the footsteps behind him of the selected member running after him, Grath took off after their target and his partner.

Mark was taking fire when Grath came running through the door and rolled to his side, firing back shots of his own and taking cover behind a crate. Mark was doing the same on the other side and then rushed forward before taking cover again.

Grath moved up, taking cover and shooting at a man who popped up behind a dumpster behind Mark. The man went down with two shots. Mark rushed forward, determined not to lose the terrorist.

Grath provided necessary cover fire for his partner while moving forward, and vice versa.

The rest of the team had caught up with them and were firing with Grath while they ran after the terrorist. A grenade exploded behind them, causing the team to dive to the ground for cover.

When Grath looked up for Mark, he had taken cover in a doorway and had taken a few shots at the terrorist, who was still running. Grath and the group turned to see more men shooting at them, walking through the smoke and burning debris that lay on the street.

With his mind on the men shooting at them, Grath reloaded and returned fire, not noticing that Mark had rushed toward the terrorist, who had run to the end of the building and around a corner.

When the gunfire ended and the men who were shooting were dead, Grath turned his attention back to his partner and their mission.

He looked around for them and started running forward, his weapon ready.

When they ran to the end of the street, making sure they weren't out in the open unless they needed to be, they turned the corner and started to run after the sound of gunshots ahead in the distance.

Catherine's group heard the explosion, and their team leader began making decisions. Two men would stay with the pilot and co-pilot they had detained, while Catherine and the two other men went toward the sound of gunshots.

They started off, running across the airfield toward the smoke that was beginning to billow into the blue sky. When they reached the scene of the grenade attack, one of the men who had been injured said that Mark and the rest of the group were up ahead. They rushed forward, running alongside the building.

Grath ran around the corner in time to see Mark fall to his knees, his chest and abdomen exploding with red spray. He looked just in time to duck back behind a corner as the terrorist turned and fired at him. Chunks of paint and stone flew off the corner in front of his face, and he ducked down, leaning around the corner and returning a few shots of his own.

The target took cover in a doorframe, and Grath took the opportunity to rush forward toward the men; he needed a better angle to hit his target.

The terrorist ducked out of the doorframe, shooting at Grath with the AK-47 as Grath rushed at him, firing his own weapon. Suddenly, the target took shots in the chest, making him drop the weapon and stumble backward through the doorway into the room beyond.

Grath looked over to see Mark had rolled onto his side, his Desert Eagle aimed at the man to protect his partner, ignoring his own bleeding chest and abdomen.

The rest of the team rushed toward their fallen comrade as Grath ran to where the terrorist had disappeared. The mission had to come first; if the target wasn't down and he went to Mark, they both could be dead.

Grath looked down in disgust at the terrorist who had caused so much harm to his country and now his partner.

The scumbag was clearly dead and looked up at Grath with empty eyes. Grath kicked the man's weapon far from his hand and left the building at a jog.

He ran to his partner, who was lying on his back as the others carefully worked to get his armored vest open so they could assess the damage. Mark's dark brown vest was coated with blood. As they carefully opened it, they saw Mark had taken at least three shots to the chest and abdomen, his vest having cracked after taking so many shots before Grath had gotten there.

Grath knelt by his partner and yelled for the combat medic who traveled with them.

The young man looked up at Grath from the other side of Mark.

"I'm right here, Grath," he said as he listened to Mark's chest with a stethoscope from the open field kit beside him. "It sounds like it went through a lung. The other shot is in the abdomen. God, he must have hit the liver some vital organ. He's bleeding too much internally. He isn't going to make it."

Grath pulled out his Desert Eagle and pointed it at the medic's face, making all movement around him halt suddenly. A few of the members who had their weapons out, looking for an external threat, quickly pointed them at Grath.

"You do something about it," he ordered, "or I will shoot you right now. Do it."

"Grath, I I can't do anything out here," the scared medic stammered. "I have nothing to perform surgery on him with. I have nothing, no tools, no --"

"Here," Grath snapped, unfolding his Gerber multi-tool one-handed and handing it to the man, his pistol still steadily pointed in the right.

The medic, along with everyone else gathered around them, looked at Grath as if he had lost it completely. When the young man hesitated, Grath switched the pistol's safety off, making the group around him tense up even more. A few took a step back, and the members who dared pull their own pistols on Grath looked at each other as if waiting for someone to tell them what to do next.

Clearly, they had never expected to be faced with the possibility of a situation like this.

Grath hadn't taken his eyes off the medic, though he saw movement from the other members out of the corners of his eyes.

"You fix whatever the hell is wrong with him. He's my partner."

A hand touched Grath's arm, which was still pointing the pistol at the medic. Grath put the safety back on the Desert Eagle and lowered it much to the relief of the group, who lowered what weapons they had drawn on the senior member.

Grath looked down at Mark's hand, then at his partner, who smiled weakly.

"We got him, didn't we?"

Grath smiled in return. "We sure did, partner. Hang in there. The doc's going to fix you up."

Mark coughed and winced; his eyes full of pain when he looked at Grath.

"Take care of Catherine for me?"

Grath was puzzled but nodded. "Mark, you aren't going to go anywhere. Just hang in there for us. They're getting the chopper right now. It'll be okay soon. Just hang in there."

Mark coughed, closing his eyes. When he opened them again, they were filled with unshed tears.

"Promise me that you will keep her safe."

Grath stared, his voice lost. He finally found it, and it came out pinched and strained, as if he were fighting back tears of his own.

"I promise, Mark, I will keep her safe. Just hang in there, buddy, we need you. We need you."

He closed his eyes and wiped some of the sweat from his forehead with the back of the hand that still held the pistol.

When he looked down again, Mark's eyes were staring straight ahead, the light inside them gone. Grath couldn't quite swallow as he put his hand over his partner's face and closed his eyes.

The sound of footsteps rushing toward them made Grath spin around, pistol drawn and ready.

When he saw Catherine running toward the group with the rest of the team, he stood up from beside Mark. A look of horror ran across her face as she recognized the fallen member, and she dropped her weapon to the ground, running faster toward them, yelling everything else forgotten.

Grath rushed to her and grabbed her around the shoulders, forcing her back away from the team from the medic checking for a pulse and finding none. The other members were quiet. Some rushed to help Grath hold Catherine as she fought to get free, screaming in horror.

Overhead, the sounds of the helicopter grew closer.

ABOUT THE AUTHOR

ML Wissing is an American writer and United States Army combat veteran. She channels her experiences into her literary works. From a young age, she has harnessed the power of words, drawing on her experiences to infuse depth and meaning into every piece she creates.

Her debut publication, *Fragments,* is a testament to her ability to infuse her writing with a deeply personal and authentic touch that resonates with readers on an emotional level. Its impact goes beyond readership, serving as a beacon of hope and healing. It is integrated into programs and curricula to showcase the transformative power of writing for soldiers and students.

Driven by her passion and the support of her loved ones, Wissing has transformed writing from a beloved hobby into a rewarding full-time career. Her dedication reflects her journey and inspires both writers and veterans, highlighting the transformative power of storytelling.

With each stroke of her pen, she crafts narratives and shapes the contours of possibility, poised to carve a remarkable legacy in literature.

She currently lives with her husband, mother-in-law, and four dogs, all of whom support her as she writes in different genres, from military poetry to realistic fiction to fantasy.

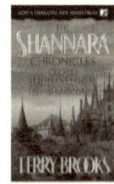